How Did We Get Here?

Throughout the history of the Church there have been few times when official changes have been made in the Mass. None of the changes, including the one we are experiencing now, ever changed the meaning of the Mass. Whatever changes and variations occurred in history, the Church always takes care to preserve the essential ritual of the breaking of the bread and the sharing of the cup.

Early Church

The earliest Christians gathered on the first day of the week, the Lord's Day, to break bread and share the cup. Depending on the community they probably prayed in their own languages: Hebrew, Aramaic, and Greek. In those early days it would have been difficult because of the number of house churches Saint Paul and the other apostles set up and the difficulty of communication to have the kind of uniform celebrations with the same prayers and weekly readings as we have today. However the apostles and their successors did develop the eucharistic celebration into the structure that we still have today. They first named it the "Breaking of the Bread" but soon they saw the need to separate the rite from a meal, both because of abuses at meals (see First Corinthians 11:17–22) and because they wanted a more prayerful setting for this act of worship. The early Jewish Christians created a Liturgy of the Word somewhat modeled after synagogue prayer that included readings from Scripture, singing of Psalms, and an instruction.

> **REFLECTION QUESTION**
> Using your responses to the *Life Experience* exercise, how do you think people in your parish will respond to the changes?

The early leaders of these communities added prayers of thanksgiving, praise, and intercession around the words of Jesus' institution. There was always a collection of goods for the poor. There is evidence from Justin Martyr, an early Church Father that tells us that a basic structure of the Mass was in place by the end of the first century. The best way to describe it is that it was a common liturgy, varied in details, but uniform in all its main points. For the most part Mass was celebrated in people's homes until the time of the Emperor Constantine (c. 306 to 337) who gave freedom to Christians and spent great sums of money building basilicas for Eucharistic worship.

Emperor Constantine

> **Read** First Corinthians 11:17–22
> If Paul had access to Twitter, how might he have written his message to the Corinthians? (Remember Twitter is 140 characters)
> Read Acts of the Apostles 20:7–10 and find the answers to the following questions.
> - How long was Paul's "Instruction"?
> - Who was Eutychus?

Latin was the language of the Roman Empire and the language of the people at that time.

Fourth Century to Sixteenth Century

Liturgy became more formalized during this period. Priests began to wear vestments. Chants and litanies emerged as did incense, bells, kissing sacred objects, and genuflection. During Medieval times with the building of beautiful cathedrals in Europe there were colorful religious processions for feasts of saints, and pilgrimages to holy shrines. During these years there is evidence that various books with Mass prayers and readings were written and used but again there were variations.

Sixteenth to Twentieth Century

It was not until the Council of Trent (1545–1563) that the Council Fathers called for a reformed Missal. In 1570, Pope Pius V responded to this call for a standard book for the celebration of Mass for the Western Church. Everything in his decree pertained to the priest celebrant and his action at the altar including the Liturgy of the Word. The Mass texts were in Latin. Although there were some modifications made between 1570 and the Second Vatican Council (1962–1965) they were not major. Most of the Mass was in Latin and it was often said that no matter where you were in the world you could enter a Catholic Church and hear the same Latin prayers.

1962–Present

The Second Vatican Council was opened by Pope John XXIII in 1962 and closed by Pope Paul VI in 1965. One of the many documents of the Council, the *Constitution on the Sacred Liturgy* (CSL), outlined some principles and guidelines for liturgical change. Among them the Council Fathers stated that the use of the Latin language should be preserved in the Latin Rites but the use of the vernacular or "mother tongue" could be used at Mass, celebration of the sacraments or other parts of the liturgy when it would be helpful for the people (see CSL, 36). It was up to

Pope John XXIII

local bishops with approval of the Holy See to decide how the vernacular would be used in their countries.

In 1963 bishops from English-speaking countries, who were in Rome for the Council, set up the International Commission on English in the Liturgy (ICEL). The Commission was started to aid the bishops in their intention to implement the Council's guide to use the vernacular language in the liturgy. For the most part the language of the Mass as you have experienced it was a result of the work of the bishops, liturgists, and theologians who translated from the first edition of *The Roman Missal* promulgated after the Second Vatican Council.

It is important to remember that the prayers of the Roman Catholic Church always originate in Latin and are then translated into the vernacular languages. There have been three Latin editions of *The Roman Missal;* the third edition of *The Roman Missal* in Latin was recently published in 2002.

GO to www.Vatican.va and search for the *Constitution on the Sacred Liturgy.*
- Read paragraph 36. Write one new thing you learned from your reading.
- Write the Latin title of the *Constitution*.

The first complete English translation dates to 1973, and some parts of the Mass first appeared in English as early as 1970. It is the third edition that has recently been translated. Translators now have a firmer grasp of the meaning of the original texts and of what is necessary to do public prayer well. The goal of this translation is to faithfully and accurately translate the Latin, without paraphrasing it. The new translation has been done to remain faithful to the Latin text. As you say and hear the new words, it is hoped you will appreciate even more the value of the faith that has been passed on to you from age to age.

What Will the New Translation Do?

The words of the Mass often refer us back to the Scriptures. The new translation will help you better connect the words of the Mass to the Scripture readings. You will see more clearly that the traditional words we use for prayer arise from expressions in the Word of God. You will also notice that the new translation uses a more formal style than we use in ordinary conversation.

REFLECTION QUESTION There are many ways to say things. You use a more formal tone with certain people than you do with your friends. Certain situations such as speaking in front of the student body or at a school debate require a different conversational style than a picnic gathering. What differences do you find in how you converse with friends, parents, or teachers?

Faithfulness to Latin
In the revised Missal many of the sentences in the prayers are longer and the vocabulary is more extensive. Longer sentences appear in English in the new translation because the previous translation broke the longer sentences up when they occurred in Latin. The new translation stitches these phrases together again. It produces prayers that express more clearly why we pray, why we hope, and how we present ourselves before God. The broader vocabulary of the new translation reflects the extensive vocabulary of Latin. For example, Latin uses a number of different words for pray, mercy, and love. As a result, the new translation uses a variety of English words and avoids the needless repetition of some words.

Translation Methods
Translators are guided by different established methods of translation. In general there are two methods. One is called *formal equivalence* and the other is *dynamic equivalence.* Those who translate the Bible and other church documents like the Latin Mass are familiar with each of these methods. The formal method uses a more literal translation. The dynamic method seeks to get across the thought that is expressed in the text. It is not as concerned about the exact words.

After the Second Vatican Council the Holy See issued an Instruction on the translation of liturgical texts which encouraged translators to follow a more dynamic approach for the revision of the Latin Mass into the vernacular. The English translation helped entire communities move from praying Mass in Latin to praying it in English. It showed us how a good translation can enhance the prayer of individuals and of entire congregations. It gave us a better understanding of the faith we share. Pope John Paul II issued a call for the revision of the texts we have been praying. In 2001, the Holy See issued *Liturgiam authenticam,* the *Fifth Instruction for the Right Implementation of the Constitution on the Sacred Liturgy of the Second Vatican Council.* This document directed translators to use the formal method in order to better connect us to the original text and to establish more unity throughout the world.

The new translation is more faithful to the original Latin text. If you've ever seen the movie version of a book you've read, you may have some idea of the challenges of translation. The movie has to be shorter. It will eliminate some characters. It will omit some of your favorite dialogue and scenes. The film may even have a different ending. People who never read the book may go to the movie and think the story is fine. But you know differently because you read the book first. You might think of ways you could have reworked the screenplay to include those things missing from the book, ways you could have improved the film. That is the kind of improvement the new translation wanted to accomplish. After a reassessment of the original text, its goal was to make the translation better.

You will see that some of the changes are small and others are considerably larger. For example, the Lord's Prayer and the Lamb of God were not changed at all. But the first part of the Gloria was completely retranslated. Some of the prayers will sound humbler. The prayers acknowledge the majesty of God and the boldness of human beings talking to the God who made us.

REFLECTION QUESTION

Choose one of the following texts: the *Gettysburg Address*, the *Declaration of Independence*, or the *Constitution of the United States of America*.

- **If you had to "translate" that document into modern day English but keep the meaning and the words as close to what the original intention of the writers was, what would you have to take into account?**
- **What does that tell you about the difficulty the translators might have encountered?**

Who Prepared the Translation?

Many people worked on the translation. The entire process was guided by the International Commission on English in the Liturgy (ICEL), the same organization that provided the first translations for all English-speaking countries a generation ago—though now with new members. Eleven bishops from different countries around the world attended the meetings. They have relied on teams of experts to propose translations that are faithful to the Latin, constant in style, and consistent in vocabulary. Individual bishops and lay people were consulted in the process. The ICEL bishops evaluated this work and made some changes to enhance it. They brought the results to the conferences of bishops whom they represent from around the world. The conferences sent their suggestions back to ICEL, which made a further round of improvements. These went back to the conferences for their vote and the submission of the texts to Rome. There, the Congregation for Divine Worship and the Discipline of the Sacraments, having consulted with the Vox Clara Committee, which is its own team of experts, made some final adjustments to the texts before approving them for publication.

This booklet was written to help you learn about and understand the changes in the revised edition of *The Roman Missal*. Whether you read this booklet at home or school, alone or with a group it is meant to help you reflect on what you are saying and doing when you gather with the assembly for Mass. As a result we hope you will come to love and appreciate the Mass even more than you do now.

Journal Questions
- How do you usually feel when things change?
- What do you love about the Mass?

The Introductory Rites

As you can see, God calls many different kinds of people. There are no age limitations in the group. They are young and not so young. Some are wealthy. Some are poor. Some are highly educated. Others are illiterate. Your best friends may be there as well as the people you find it difficult to like. There may be people who speak a different language than you speak. No matter what the descriptions and variety of people you observe are, they are all gathered for one reason.

When we gather for Mass we are called a liturgical assembly of faithful people who are gathered to give God thanks and praise for all the gifts he has given us. The whole assembly gathers to give praise and thanks to God. When the assembly gathers, God, the Father, Son, and Holy Spirit is present.

Life Experience

With a partner or in a small group, describe the diversity in your parish community. Use your responses to the following questions as conversation starters

- If you were to take even the most basic demographic survey of the people who were at Mass with you last Sunday, what do you think you would find?
- List the possibilities of similarities and differences you might find in the group.

The Introductory Rites gather us as an assembly. They help us focus on why we are here.

Entrance Procession and Chant

The Mass begins when we stand and the procession begins. Standing is an act of honor. If a very important person came into a room and started to talk with you, you would stand up as a sign of respect. We believe that Christ is present as our community begins its prayer. On Sundays the priest and the other ministers usually come into the church in a procession which starts at the rear of the church. Signs and symbols of our faith are carried in the procession. Someone carries the processional cross. The Cross reminds us of Jesus' sacrifice for us on the Cross and his death and Resurrection. The deacon or one of the lectors carries the *Book of the Gospels* which contains all the Gospels that are read at Sunday Mass. We honor it because it contains the words of Christ.

In most parishes we usually sing a song or hymn during the procession. This hymn replaces a one-sentence antiphon that appears in *The Roman Missal* for the Mass of the day. It is called the Entrance Chant. The antiphon in *The Roman Missal* is usually a Scripture verse. There is a different antiphon for every Mass. Whether we sing the song or pray aloud the antiphon, it helps us think about why we are here to pray. In many parishes when you go to Mass during the week all the people recite the words of the antiphon together. In other parishes, only the priest or reader will pray the words.

Research an Entrance Chant Using *The Sacramentary* (or the new edition of *The Roman Missal,* if available), worship aid, or an online resource find the Entrance Chant for next Sunday.

The Sign of the Cross

When the priest, the deacon, and the other ministers enter the sanctuary they bow to the altar. We reverence the altar by bowing because the altar is a symbol of Christ himself. After they bow, the priest and deacon kiss the altar. Sometimes the priest will incense the cross and the altar.

The priest says the words for the Sign of the Cross and we answer "Amen." When he says "In the name of the Father, and of the Son, and of the Holy Spirit" we also make a gesture with our right hand. We sign ourselves. All of us make the Sign of the Cross together. The gesture of signing is our way of saying we belong to God. The Sign of the Cross also reminds us that Jesus died on the Cross for us.

The Greeting

Following the Sign of the Cross, the priest welcomes the assembly with a greeting. At this point when the priest greets us it is not the same as saying "Hi" or "Good morning." When we respond it is not the same as meeting the priest on the street and saying "Hi, Father, how are you." The following options remind us that the Risen Christ is here with us and we are now entering a holy time of prayer. The greeting is formal and uses scriptural language and the priest greets the assembly in his sacramental role as celebrant not in his role as the everyday priest we might meet in the parking lot or at school. We too are in a different role. We are there as a member of a worshipping praying faith community.

The priest welcomes the assembly with a greeting.

REFLECTION QUESTION How does identifying yourself as "being a member of a worshipping praying faith community" differ from identifying yourself as 'being a Catholic kid who goes to Mass on Sunday'

Each of the three greetings has its roots in Scripture.

The First Option

> The grace of our Lord Jesus Christ,
> and the love of God,
> and the communion of the Holy Spirit
> be with you all.

This greeting is a direct quote from Paul's Second Letter to the Corinthians (see 2 Corinthians 13:13). Think of this greeting as a wish that Paul is making for the Corinthians; a blessing he is giving. He wishes the community grace. Grace is God's life in us and the source of our freedom from sin and death. He wishes the community the love of God. Finally he wishes the community communion through the Holy Spirit. Communion being the fellowship and unity they are called to live in as a community. Paul prays that grace, love, and communion be given by God, the Father, Son, and Holy Spirit to the whole community. When this apostolic greeting is used at the beginning of the liturgy, the Church prays that these same gifts of the Christian life be given to the community it is addressed to.

The Second Option

> Grace to you and peace from God our Father
> and the Lord Jesus Christ.

This text is the second option for the greeting. Paul uses this greeting as part of the introduction to many of his letters (see Romans 1:7). You may remember that Paul was a Jew and a Roman citizen. He was the apostle to the Gentiles, those who were not Jews. With this greeting Paul combines a Greek greeting, grace (*charis*) and the ancient Hebrew blessing, peace (*shalom*). For Paul, this is a Christian greeting of unity in Christ. He does not separate Jewish and Gentile believers. Instead he addresses them together, as members of the one Church.

When you reflected on your community previously you noticed obvious differences. You may also be aware of divisions in your parish or between friends and family members who are worshipping together. Paul wrote to communities who were often divided and not being very loving toward each other. Just as our communities sometimes are today. His greeting was a concrete reminder to them that they were called to be a united body of Christ. They were called and given the grace to be transformed in Christ. Just as we are today.

When this greeting is used to welcome people at Mass it proclaims something we do not often think about because we are lulled to accept the status quo. It says that the Church is not like any other social group. Yes, we have our differences, there are divisions but by faith we are called to oneness in Christ and by acting with God's grace we can be transformed. We live in a culture that has deep divisions of race, class, gender, politics, and economic levels. They exist in our parish communities too. We believe that our common identity as Christians transcends our differences. With this greeting at

Paul's greeting is a concrete reminder that all are called to be a united body of Christ.

the beginning of the Mass, the Church appeals to us to treat one another with love—to extend grace and to make peace with one another. That is how we become witnesses of Christ to the world.

REFLECTION QUESTION What do you think or feel about discord and division among Christians?

The Third Option

The Lord be with you.

This greeting is a common greeting throughout the Bible. Our ancestors used the words "The Lord be with you" to greet people and to cheer them up (see Ruth 2:4; 2 Chronicles 15:2). When the angel Gabriel came to greet Mary he said, "The Lord is with you" (Luke 1:28). When we hear the words "The Lord be with you" we remember that Jesus told his followers he would always be with them (see Matthew 28:20). This liturgical greeting, "The Lord be with you," connects us with God's faithful people in both the Old and New Testament.

REFLECTION QUESTION Think about how many different ways people use the word "spirit": "He has a real spirit; She has such spirit. That's the spirit. They have great team spirit." Spirit is more than the physical person. It is greater than the sum of the parts of a team.

The Response

The people's response to all three of these options is "And with your spirit." "And with your spirit" is one of the responses that has changed with the translation. We used to say "And also with you." "And with your spirit" is inspired by passages that conclude four of Paul's letters. At the end of his letter to the Philippians, Paul writes: "The grace of the Lord Jesus Christ be with your spirit" (Philippians 4:23). He ends his second letter to his friend Timothy by saying: "The Lord be with your spirit" (2 Timothy 4:22). In Galatians 6:18 he says "May the grace of our Lord Jesus Christ be with your spirit, brothers and sisters. Amen." To Philemon and his community he says: "The grace of the Lord Jesus Christ be with your spirit" (Philemon 25). In almost every case, Paul addresses the words to the Christian community, not to one minister or member. The two

> **Read** the following Bible passages and write a description of spirit as you understand it from a Biblical perspective.
>
> Deuteronomy 34: 9 2 Kings 2:9
> Psalm 34:18 Ezekiel 11:19

parts of the greeting express a desire that the Lord be present to the spirit of the entire community.

Throughout his writings Paul urges his readers to take on the spirit of Christ. For example:

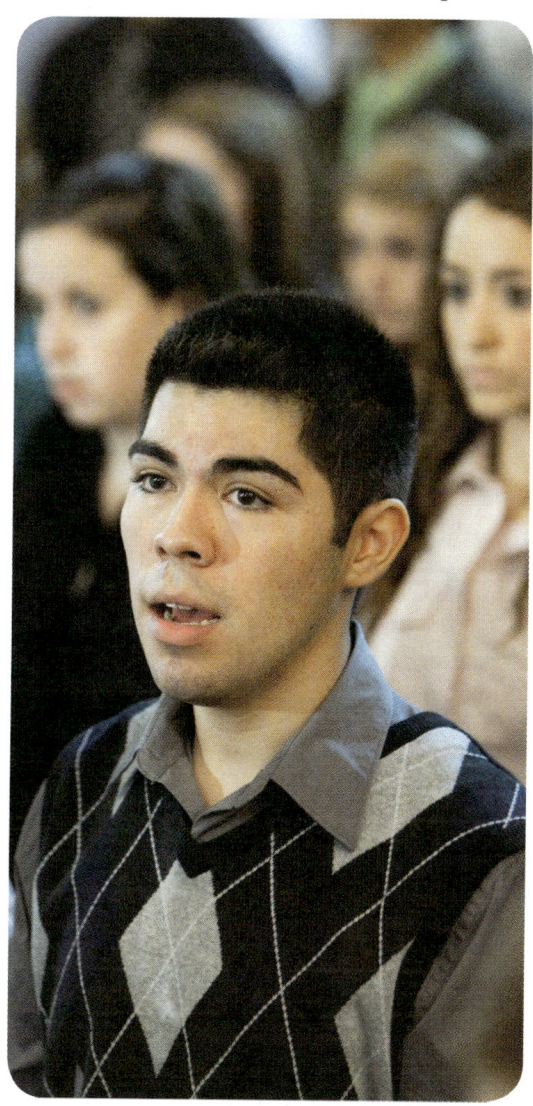

The two parts of the greeting express a desire that the Lord be present to the spirit of the entire community.

> But now we are discharged from the law, dead to that which held us captive, so that we are slaves not under the old written code but in the new life of the Spirit.
> Romans 7:6

> But anyone united to the Lord becomes one spirit with him.
> 1 Corinthians 6:17

The two parts of this greeting express a desire that the Lord be present to the spirit of the entire community. Based on evidence from Paul's letters, the priest's line could imply, "The Lord be with your spirit," and the people's line would then reciprocate: "and with your spirit." Because this brief dialogue at the beginning of Mass is begun only by an ordained priest or Bishop, the reply also affirms that the Holy Spirit has come to the priest or Bishop in a special way. The dialogue establishes the interdependence of the priest and the people as they take up their roles to praise God.

REFLECTION QUESTION In what ways do you see your parish community living in the spirit of Christ?

Penitential Act

After the greeting the priest invites us to ask God for mercy. *Mercy* means "kindness" and "forgiveness." Also a merciful person is willing to help people who are in need. When we ask for God's mercy during this part of Mass we recognize our sinfulness and we trust that God in his kindness is ready to forgive us and make us one with him. We admit that we are in need of God's help. *Penitential* means "to show we are sorry for having done something bad." During the Penitential Act we show our sorrow for our sins through words and actions.

The priest can choose from three different ways to pray during the Penitential Act. Each of the choices begins with the priest calling us to prepare.

The priest says:

Brethren (brothers and sisters), let us acknowledge our sins, and so prepare ourselves to celebrate the
sacred mysteries.

After the priest greets us we are quiet. The time of silence is an opportunity to think about why we need God's mercy.

The First Option

The first option is to pray the *Confiteor*. The *Confiteor* is a prayer of confession. *Confession* means "to admit something." When we pray the *Confiteor* we pray aloud together. We admit our sinfulness. We ask for God's mercy:

Previous Translation	New Translation
I confess to almighty God, and to you, my brothers and sisters, that I have **sinned through my own fault** They strike their breast: in my thoughts and in my words, in what I have done, and in what I have failed to do; **and** I ask blessed Mary, ever virgin, all the angels and saints, and you, my brothers and sisters, to pray for me to the Lord, our God.	I confess to almighty God and to you, my brothers and sisters, that I have **greatly sinned,** in my thoughts and in my words, in what I have done and in what I have failed to do, And, striking their breast, they say: **through my fault, through my fault, through my most grievous fault;** Then they continue: **therefore** I ask blessed Mary ever-Virgin, all the Angels and Saints, and you, my brothers and sisters, to pray for me to the Lord our God.

At first, saying the phrase "I have greatly sinned," striking our breast at "through my fault," repeating those words, and then adding, "through my most grievous fault," may make it look as though we are a lot more sinful now than we used to be. But that is not why the change was made.

> **Read** both translations of the **Confiteor**. With a friend or in a small group discuss and compare your responses to the following questions:
> - What are the changes in the prayer?
> - What feelings do you have about the changed text?

It was made to keep closer to the Latin words. Remember, that is one of the guiding principles of the translation. It is a closer faithfulness to the words in Latin—not a sharper analysis of our sinfulness. At the same time it does express more clearly the seriousness of our sin and the sincerity of our contrition. The *Confiteor* still concludes with the "Lord, have mercy," and we may still use "Kyrie, eleison" instead.

At the conclusion of the *Confiteor* we admit that we need and want others to pray to God to be merciful to us. We pray for one another.

The Second Option

The second choice for the Penitential Act in *The Roman Missal* is the shortest. The priest will first invite us to prepare ourselves in silence (refer to his prayer on page 8). Then the prayer continues. See the chart below.

The new translation points to Old Testament roots. The first phrases come from Baruch 3:2, the second comes from Psalm 85:8. These verses are to be followed by the "Lord, have mercy" or "Kyrie, eleison."

Previous Translation	New Translation
Priest: Lord, we have sinned against you: Lord, have mercy.	**Priest:** Have mercy on us, O Lord.
People: Lord, have mercy.	**People:** For we have sinned against you.
Priest: Lord, show us your mercy and love.	**Priest:** Show us, O Lord, your mercy.
People: And grant us your salvation.	**People:** And grant us your salvation.

The Third Option

The option many of us are familiar with is the third choice. In that choice we pray three invocations ending with "Lord, have mercy," "Christ, have mercy," and then "Lord, have mercy" again. We repeat the ending phrase after the priest. If the priest uses the Greek words for the "Lord, have mercy," "Kyrie, eleison," "Christe, eleison," and "Kyrie, eleison." We respond with those words.

Before the Penitential Act ends, the priest proclaims a prayer of absolution, a prayer for forgiveness or pardon. This prayer of absolution is different from and does not take the place of the absolution we receive in the Sacrament of Penance. The priest will use the same prayer you are used to hearing at Mass:

Priest: May almighty God have mercy on us,
forgive us our sins,
and bring us to everlasting life.

People: **Amen.**

These choices may be replaced with the Rite of Blessing and Sprinkling of Water. Many parishes choose to do this during Christmas and Easter Time.

The Rite of Blessing and Sprinkling of water may replace the Penitential Act. This rite reminds us of our Baptism.

Kyrie

The Kyrie, eleison (Lord, have mercy) follows the Penitential Act, unless we have done the third choice above. Just like that choice, we respond "Lord, have mercy. Christ, have mercy. Lord, have mercy." But, there are no invocations.

Gloria

One of the biggest changes you'll notice in the new prayers of the Mass is the words of the Gloria.

The chart on the next page shows you how the text of this hymn has changed. Notice the words in bold print.

The word *glory* translates the Hebrew word *kabod*. When *kabod* is used about people it means honor and importance. The Gloria is a joyful hymn of praise and honor to God. When we say or sing it we honor God's importance. We praise God because God is worthy of all honor.

The Gloria was written by our ancestors over a long period of time. If we were going to write a prayer or a poem we might consult a dictionary. Our ancestors consulted the Bible for the words and phrases they wanted to use.

Previous Translation	New Translation
Glory to God in the highest, and **peace to his people on earth.**	Glory to God in the highest, and **on earth peace to people of good will.**
Lord God, heavenly King, **almighty God and Father, we worship you, we give you thanks, we praise you for your glory.**	**We praise you, we bless you, we adore you, we glorify you, we give you thanks for your great glory, Lord God, heavenly King, O God, almighty Father.**
Lord Jesus Christ, **only Son of the Father,** Lord God, Lamb of God, you take away the sin of the world: have mercy on us; you are seated at the right hand of the Father: **receive our prayer.**	Lord Jesus Christ, **Only Begotten Son,** Lord God, Lamb of God, **Son of the Father,** you take away the sins of the world, have mercy on us; **you take away the sins of the world, receive our prayer;** you are seated at the right hand of the Father, **have mercy on us.**
For you alone are the Holy One, you alone are the Lord, you alone are the Most High, Jesus Christ, with the Holy Spirit, in the glory of God the Father. Amen.	For you alone are the Holy One, you alone are the Lord, you alone are the Most High, Jesus Christ, with the Holy Spirit, in the glory of God the Father. Amen.

The Gloria begins with the words of the angels who sang God's praise at the birth of Jesus.

All through the Bible we hear that God showed his glory to his people. The words mean that God made himself visible and present to people.

Moses saw and showed God's glory:

> Now the appearance of the glory of the LORD was like a devouring fire on the top of the mountain in the sight of the people of Israel.
>
> Exodus 24:17

> Moses came down from Mount Sinai. As he came down from the mountain with the two tablets of the covenant in his hand, Moses did not know that the skin of his face shone because he had been talking with God.
>
> Exodus 34:29

In the Gospel according to John we read that the people who saw Jesus saw his glory. In Jesus they saw God made visible.

> And the Word became flesh and lived among us, and we have seen his glory, the glory as of a father's only son, full of grace and truth.
>
> John 1:14

God has done great things for us. He gave us life, a world to live in, the beauty of creation and his only Son. In all these things God shows himself to us. He is present to us. When we look around at all God has created we are in awe. The Gloria is the Church's song of awe and praise of God who continues to show himself to us. We say or sing the Gloria on all Sundays of the year, except for those during Advent and Lent, or if All Souls Day (November 2) falls on a Sunday.

Sometimes when we are really excited about something we talk and talk. We are so excited we can't stop and we use lots of words to describe our excitement. The first part of the Gloria is a prayer like that. As an assembly we are so excited about the ways God shows himself to us that "we praise," "bless," "adore," "glorify," and give him "thanks for [his] great glory."

The new translation changed "his people on earth" to "people of good will." This is an example of

The Gloria is the Church's song of awe and praise of God.

"We give you thanks for your great glory."

how the translators let the English express more literally the sentiments of the Latin original. The previous text describes the people as belonging to God. The revision describes their quality "of good will." The phrase is faithful to the original Latin prayer and better connects with the familiar Christmas story we hear in the Gospel according to Luke at the birth of Jesus.

"We praise you, / we bless you, / we adore you, / we glorify you, / we give you thanks for your great glory, / Lord God, heavenly King, / O God, almighty Father." This replaced a shorter text in the previous version. The one we had been singing probably abbreviated this section because it seemed a bit excessive. Now all the descriptions for God have been restored, and the result is excessive—but that is the point. We are so overcome with awe in the presence of God that we keep searching for words to describe the experience, and the result—word upon word—seems the best way to demonstrate the overwhelming experience of meeting God in prayer.

In the second part of the prayer we continue by giving praise and Glory to God the Son. We call Jesus the "Only Begotten Son." When we say or sing that Jesus is the "Only Begotten Son" of God. We are not saying Jesus is just another son of God. "Only" means "one of a kind." Jesus is not adopted. He is the same nature as the Father. He truly is one of a kind. In Baptism we are made *adopted* children of God.

We give God praise for his Son, Jesus.

When we pray this hymn we say that Jesus takes "away the sins of the world." We know that Jesus takes away original sin and our own personal sins. At the words "you take away the sins of the world," the phrases appear in a different order in the new translation, to imitate the order of the words in Latin. A small change appears in this line. We have been singing about "sin" in the singular, but the new translation has "sins" in the plural. The difference indicates that Jesus takes away not just generic sin from the world, but individual sin. He forgives people their personal sins. In Latin, the word for sins is in the plural. The Gloria gives us words to praise God and affirm the forgiving power of Jesus Christ.

Collect or Opening Prayer

The Introductory Rites conclude with the Collect, which had been previously referred to as the Opening Prayer of the Mass. When you first see the word *Collect* you might think of collecting or gathering things such as stones. When the priest prays the Collect he is gathering the prayers of the whole assembly and addressing them to God.

The priest does not make up his own prayers for the Collects. They are already in *The Roman Missal*. The priest extends his hands as he prays. That gesture reminds us that he is gathering us and all our prayers. All the Collects

The priest extends his hands when he prays, gathering all our prayers.

have been completely retranslated, and they will sound a little different to you. The sentences are longer and more complex and may be difficult to follow at first. However, over a short period of time your ear should tune in to the flow of the prayer and make it easier for your heart to join its intention. Listen carefully as the priest prays the prayer. When he is finished you will notice another change in the first translation, the Opening Prayer ended with a formula that usually began, "We ask this through our Lord Jesus Christ." Now you will notice that the conclusion will make the role of the Persons of the Trinity more precise. The assembly concludes the Collect with the word "Amen," just as we have been doing. When we say "Amen" we are saying: "Yes, I believe." Our "Amen" solemnly affirms our belief in God and the unity of the prayers of everyone present. Then we sit and prepare ourselves to hear the Word of God.

Journal Questions

- Create a word map of the parts of Chapter 2 that gave you something to think about for your own spiritual growth.
- Describe your feelings about the meaning of the Introductory Rites in a poem or a letter to God.

Ch. 3

The Liturgy of the Word

We now begin the first of the two major parts of the Mass. It is called the Liturgy of the Word. We work with the word by:

- Listening carefully to the three readings and the Psalm, which are all taken from Scripture.
- Paying attention to what we hear in the homily. The homily is given by a priest or deacon and helps us understand better how we can apply the Sunday readings and liturgy to our lives.
- Asking the Holy Spirit to open our hearts to God's message.
- Deciding how we can live the message of the day's readings in our life.

Life Experience

With a partner or in a small group describe the importance of books, stories, and words in your life. Use your responses to the following questions to develop your description.

- Which book, story, or poem was your favorite as a child?
- In what way has that book, story, or poem influenced you? The way you think or act?
- What is your favorite Scripture story? Why is it your favorite?

Just because we sit and listen for most of the first part of the Liturgy of the Word does not mean we are not doing anything.

During the Liturgy of the Word as each of the first two readings end the reader will say "The word of the Lord," and we answer, "Thanks be to God." Between these first two Scripture readings we sing a Psalm. The Psalm is usually sung by a cantor. The reader uses the *Lectionary for Mass* to proclaim the readings. The Lectionary contains all the readings for Masses celebrated on Sundays, feast days, and weekdays.

There are virtually no changes to the English texts we use for the Liturgy of the Word. The major changes affect the Creed or Profession of Faith. However, there are some minor changes.

The words that precede and conclude the proclamation of the Gospel have changed. If a deacon is assisting, he

The *Book of the Gospels* is a sacred book.

goes to the priest and asks for a blessing. The words they say to each other have a slightly different translation, although the meaning is the same. The priest has been praying that the deacon may "worthily proclaim" the Gospel, and in the new text he says:

May the Lord be in your heart and on your lips,
that you may proclaim his Gospel worthily and well,
in the name of the Father, and of the Son, ✚ and of the Holy Spirit.

If the priest proclaims the Gospel, he offers a short prayer in a low voice. The word order of that text is slightly different, and in it he calls the proclamation God's "holy Gospel"—not just the "Gospel." He prays:

Cleanse my heart and my lips, almighty God,
that I may worthily proclaim your holy Gospel.

All these prayers are said quietly. You may never have heard them aloud before, and you probably will not hear these changes as they are spoken. Several times at Mass the priest and the deacon say some prayers in a low voice. They are saying these extra prayers to center their minds on the meaning of their actions.

When the priest or deacon stands at the ambo and greets you, he will still say, "The Lord be with you," but your response will now be, "And with your spirit." This follows the practice established in the Introductory Rites of the Mass.

> **What are two ways you can center your mind to listen to the Gospel and the homily?**

When the Gospel is announced, we say, "Glory to you, O Lord." And at the conclusion of the Gospel we say, "Praise to you, Lord Jesus Christ." We sometimes use the word "O" before words such as "Lord" and "God" in sentences that are prayers. Doing so makes the prayer more beautiful, poetic, and respectful to God.

After this, the priest or deacon kisses the book. Kissing the book is another sign of honor and reverence for God's holy word. The *Book of the Gospels* is a sacred book. Then the priest or deacon says this short prayer in a low voice: "Through the words of the Gospel / may our sins be wiped away."

For the homily, the preacher still observes the same expectations for its preparation. Normally you hear a homily based on the scripture texts that helps us think about how we can live the Scriptures in our daily life. However, the priest or deacon may preach about any of the texts of Mass. Especially as the new translation is put into practice, you may hear some homilies about parts of the Mass such as the Gloria, the Creed, or the Eucharistic Prayer.

The Profession of Faith

Another word for the Profession of Faith is Creed. A Creed is a short statement of a person or community's beliefs. The word *Creed* comes from the Latin word *Credo* which means "I believe." When we say *Credo* or "I believe" we pledge our loyalty to something or someone.

When we say the Creed during Mass we are expressing our faith in God, the Father, the Son, and the Holy Spirit. We are expressing our loyalty to all that the Church believes and teaches. The words Christians used to profess their beliefs changed over time but the beliefs always stayed the same. In the very beginning of the Church our Creed was the very short statement "Jesus is Lord." As the Church grew, Church leaders added other statements and the Creed grew. Even though we use different words when we pray the Nicene Creed and the Apostles' Creed they both say what we believe.

Every Sunday all around the world Catholics profess the Creed in various languages. When the Creed is translated into any language, the person who is doing the translation always uses the same Latin words that other translators use. The guiding principle for the new translation has been to make the English closer to the Latin original. Translators have learned a lot in the past

The Creed Americans usually say is the Nicene Creed.

forty years and they have given us a text that expresses our common faith with more precision. Especially for this part of Mass, it is important that we all say the same thing no matter what language we are speaking, because we are one Church and there is one faith. "There is one body and one Spirit, just as you were called to the one hope of your calling, one Lord, one faith, one baptism, one God and Father of all, who is above all and through all and in all" (Ephesians 4:4–6).

Nicene Creed

The Creed Americans usually proclaim on Sunday is the Nicene Creed. Sometimes it may be replaced with the Apostles' Creed. The Nicene Creed was formulated at the Council of Nicaea in 325 AD. The Council was called by the Emperor Constantine who elevated Christianity to favored status in the Roman empire. "One God, one Lord, one faith, one church, one empire, one emperor" became his motto. When he discovered that "one faith and one church" were being fractured by theological disputes, especially conflicting understandings of the nature of Christ, he convened the Council of Nicaea which began to develop clear articles of faith. As a result of prayer and discussion by the bishops and theologians at both the Council of Nicaea and the Council of Constantinople which occurred in 381 AD the Nicene Creed was developed.

Previous Translation	New Translation
We believe in one God, the Father, the Almighty, maker of heaven and earth, **of all that is seen and unseen.**	**I believe** in one God, the Father almighty, maker of heaven and earth, **of all things visible and invisible.**
We believe in one Lord, Jesus Christ, **the only** Son of God, **eternally begotten of the Father,** God from God, Light from Light, true God from true God, begotten, not made, **one in Being with the Father.** Through him all things were made. For us men and for our salvation he came down from heaven:	**I believe** in one Lord Jesus Christ, **the Only Begotten** Son of God, **born of the Father before all ages.** God from God, Light from Light, true God from true God, begotten, not made, **consubstantial with the Father;** through him all things were made. For us men and for our salvation he came down from heaven,
All bow during these two lines:	At the words that follow, up to and including and became man, all bow.
by the power of the Holy Spirit he was born of the Virgin Mary, and became man.	**and by the Holy Spirit was incarnate of the Virgin Mary,** and became man.
For our sake he was crucified under Pontius Pilate; **he suffered, died, and was buried. On the third day he rose again in fulfillment of the Scriptures;** he ascended into heaven and is seated at the right hand of the Father. He will come again in glory to judge the living and the dead, and his kingdom will have no end.	For our sake he was crucified under Pontius Pilate, **he suffered death and was buried, and rose again on the third day in accordance with the Scriptures.** He ascended into heaven and is seated at the right hand of the Father. He will come again in glory to judge the living and the dead and his kingdom will have no end.
We believe in the Holy Spirit, the Lord, the giver of life, who proceeds from the Father and the Son. With the Father and the Son he is **worshipped** and glorified. **He** has spoken through the Prophets. **We believe in** one holy catholic and apostolic Church. **We acknowledge** one baptism for the forgiveness of sins. **We look for** the resurrection of the dead, and the life of the world to come. Amen.	**I believe** in the Holy Spirit, the Lord, the giver of life, who proceeds from the Father and the Son, **who** with the Father and the Son is **adored** and glorified, **who** has spoken through the prophets. **I believe in** one, holy, catholic and apostolic Church. **I confess** one Baptism for the forgiveness of sins **and I look forward to** the resurrection of the dead and the life of the world to come. Amen.

"And by the Holy Spirit was incarnate of the Virgin Mary, / and became man."

"I believe." The Creed begins with "I" instead of "We." The Creed is still the faith of all of us, but when we say "I" each of us takes responsibility to proclaim our faith together with other believers. I make a promise or commitment with the rest of the assembly.

The Creed is still the faith of the entire Church, but each of us proclaims it to assert our personal faith together with other believers. "I believe" is a literal translation of the Latin word *Credo,* and it is consistent with the translation that has been used in many other countries around the world since the Second Vatican Council.

"Of all things visible and invisible." The choice of these words over "seen and unseen" makes this line a little more

> With a partner or in a small group develop a skit around a specific event where a young person took responsibility to proclaim their faith in front of their peers.

27

precise. Some things that are visible by nature are actually unseen at certain times and places. Your relatives who live across the country are visible, but unseen to you. Your great-great grandfather was visible once upon a time, but now he is unseen. We believe that God is the maker not only of things we cannot see for whatever reason, but also of things that are in fact invisible—for example, the angels who occupy a place in our belief and worship.

"Only Begotten." We saw these words in the Gloria. They replace the word "only," and they translate the Latin more fully. They mean we believe that Jesus is really "one of a kind." We believe he always was. He did not start when he was in Mary's womb. He was always the Son of God. His presence has always been part of the divine plan.

"I believe in one Lord Jesus Christ, / the Only Begotten Son of God, / born of the Father before all ages."

"Born of the Father before all ages." These words replace "eternally begotten of the Father," and makes them more precise. Their source is in John's account of the Gospel: "In the beginning was the Word, and the Word was with God, and the Word was God. He was in the beginning with God" (John 1:1–2).These words make it clear that we believe Jesus lived with the Father before time began. Colossians 1:15 also probably inspired this expression, "He is the image of the invisible God, the firstborn of all creation. . . ." "Firstborn" in Colossians is equal to "begotten of the Father."

"Consubstantial." This is a big word. It means that Jesus and his Father are one and the same God. Jesus is not like any other human being because he is human and divine. It replaces the expression "one in Being," and it describes the relationship between Jesus and the Father. In the previous translation, "one in Being" was thought to be more understandable and closer to the original Greek of the Creed. However, the new translation chooses a word that lies closer to the Latin equivalent, *consubstantialis*. The question of how Jesus relates to the Father has immense importance. Heresies have divided Christians over this very issue. The early Church councils used words that carefully articulated orthodox faith, and they chose this word to express the dogma of Jesus' divinity. The Latin word means having the same substance, which is even more fundamental than "one in Being." "Consubstantial" is a very unusual word. We don't use it for anything else. But it is describing a very unusual thing—the nature of the relationship between Jesus Christ and his Father. Human words will never be able to perfectly describe the mystery of God.

We bow at the words of the Incarnation.

"Incarnate." This word replaces the word "born" in the previous translation. It means something like given flesh. It states our belief that the Word became flesh in the womb of the Virgin Mary. The previous translation could be misunderstood to state that the Word became flesh when Jesus was born. That is not our faith. Jesus was not simply born by the power of the Holy Spirit; he was conceived that way. In both translations this phrase is followed by this statement: "and became man." The new translation makes it clearer that Jesus did not become a human when he was born; he was incarnate in the womb, and in that event "became man."

"Suffered death." These words replace the verbs "suffered, died" in the previous translation. Literally the Latin says he suffered and was buried, and the word suffered implies his dying. Because the verb died is not there in Latin, "suffered death" seems a better way to express what happened to Jesus. The point is because Jesus really died we know his Resurrection is real.

"In accordance with the Scriptures." These words replace "in fulfillment of the Scriptures." In Latin, the word more nearly means "in accordance with" or even "according to." The new translation broadens the meaning of the word Scriptures and the role they play in our faith.

"Adored." The new translation chooses this word to replace "worshipped." We believe that God should be respected and highly praised in a way proper only to God.

"I confess." In the Creed the word, "confess" means "profess belief in." When we say "I confess " we are saying we believe with all our heart. This replaces "We acknowledge," and is a more forceful expression. In this context,

29

"confess" means profess belief in—not express sorrow for sins. It sounds stronger than "acknowledge" because it involves the heart, not just the head.

"I look forward to the resurrection." At the end of the Creed, instead of saying merely that we "look for the resurrection," we say we "look forward to" it. This is a clearer translation of the Latin, but it also resounds with confidence. We are saying that we are really sure that we can live with God forever.

> Take some time to write your own Creed based on the Nicene Creed. When you write your Creed, include sentences on God the Father, Jesus Christ, and the Holy Spirit. Discuss your Creed in class or at home.

Prayer of the Faithful

After the Creed, the Liturgy of the Word concludes with the Prayer of the Faithful. The first English translation included samples, and new versions of these are appearing in the new edition of *The Roman Missal*. But the entire text of the Prayer of the Faithful may be freely composed in your local community. In many parishes these prayers are written ahead of time by members of the assembly. Church leaders expect that our parish communities know best what we should pray for. The Prayer of the Faithful will be different from week to week. This part of Mass enjoys the greatest flexibility.

When these petitions are written they always include these four areas:

- What are the needs of the whole Church and public authorities?
- What does the world need to turn from sin and toward God?
- Who is burdened by any kind of difficulty?
- What are the needs of the local community?

> With a partner or in a small group write the Prayer of the Faithful for one of the areas above.

Over the years different parts and prayers included in the Liturgy of the Word may change but the Word of God will never change. It will always draw us closer to God and call us to be his followers. It will always help us see how God wants us to live as his Chosen People.

Journal Questions

- In what ways do you "work" with the Word?
- When has a homily or Scripture passage helped you deepen your relationship with God?

The Liturgy of the Eucharist

Now begins the second of the two important parts of the Mass. It is called the Liturgy of the Eucharist. Remember that the word *liturgy* comes from a Greek word that means "the public worship of the whole Church." In the Liturgy of the Eucharist we as members of the assembly are called to do the public work of thanking God for his many gifts and especially the gift of his Son Jesus.

Presentation and Preparation of the Gifts

The Liturgy of the Eucharist begins with the Presentation and Preparation of the Gifts. During this part of the Mass the priest

Life Experience

With a partner or in a small group describe the importance of gratitude in your life. Use your responses to the following questions as conversation starters.

- List 10 things you are grateful for.
- How do you feel after you have done someone a favor and they do not thank you?
- How many different ways do people give thanks?

prepares the altar and the gifts of bread and wine which will become the Body and Blood of Christ. In some parishes, a hymn is sung as the gifts are collected and the altar is prepared. These gifts will be placed on the altar. Once the priest has received the gifts and stands at the altar, he praises God, who has provided them. This part of Mass is brief, and there will be only a very few changes to the words when we start using the new translation.

"Blessed." The priest says two prayers one over the bread and one over the wine. Both times he says: "Blessed are you, Lord God of all creation." To each of these prayers when a hymn is not sung, we respond: "Blessed be God forever." We often ask God to bless us. During this part of the Mass we are calling God blessed. The word *blessed* means "holy" or "sacred."

"Sacrifice." The priest washes his hands and then he invites us to pray. He says:

> Pray, brethren (brothers and sisters),
> that my sacrifice and yours
> may be acceptable to God,
> the almighty Father.

> The people rise and reply:

> May the Lord accept the sacrifice at your hands
> for the praise and glory of his name,
> for our good
> and the good of all his holy Church.

To *sacrifice* means "to give something up." Jesus gave up his life for us on the Cross. We believe that the Mass is the same sacrifice as Jesus made. *Sacrifice* also means "to make holy." Our sacrifices bring us closer to God. They make us holy. When we pray this prayer we join our sacrifices to Jesus' sacrifice in the Mass. We want God to accept our sacrifices.

> Make a list of sacrifices young people make for their good or the good of the Church.

The Eucharistic Prayer

The Eucharistic Prayer is the center and summit of the Mass. It is the great prayer of thanksgiving and sanctification. The priest invites us to lift up our hearts in prayer. We unite our thoughts with those expressed by the priest, who addresses God in the name of the entire community. Together with the priest we all join ourselves with Christ to proclaim the marvelous deeds of

The Eucharistic Prayer is the center and summit of the Mass.

God. During the Eucharistic Prayer, the priest speaks more words than we do. At the beginning of the Eucharistic Prayer we exchange a dialogue with the priest celebrant as we sing the Holy, Holy, Holy and the Memorial Acclamation. We conclude the Eucharistic Prayer with the great Amen. But the rest of the time we listen and pray in silence. It is important to pay attention to the prayers the priest says on our behalf.

There is more than one Eucharistic Prayer. The new translation has affected the entire collection of Eucharistic Prayers. Prior to the Second Vatican Council there was only one Eucharistic Prayer. It is still in the Missal (Eucharistic Prayer I) and it is especially appropriate on Sundays, on days when we celebrate any of the saints mentioned in the prayer, and on days when a special phrase denoting the nature of the celebration may be inserted into it—such as Christmas, Holy Thursday, and the octave of Easter. Three more Eucharistic Prayers were added to this one right after the Second Vatican Council. Eucharistic Prayer II is the shortest of them and was designed especially for weekday Mass. It is based on a prayer that dates to the third century.

Eucharistic Prayer III was composed following Vatican II, and it is also appropriate for Sundays and feast days. Eucharistic Prayer IV is based on a fourth-century prayer from the Eastern Tradition of the Church. It has its own Preface that gives a fuller summary of salvation history. It was intended for use during Ordinary Time. In addition, some Eucharistic Prayers were composed for special circumstances. Two which were written as part of the Holy Year of 1975 express the theme of reconciliation, and are often used during Lent. Another Eucharistic Prayer was composed for Masses for Various Needs and Occasions. It is used at Masses which are celebrated for different intentions, ranging from civil authorities to favorable weather.

In the Liturgy of the Eucharist, the changes in the translation will affect what you hear more than what you say. In time, as you listen and pay attention you will grow in your ability to unite your thoughts with those of the entire community, and with Christ, as you give thanks and praise to God.

> **G O** online (www.usccb.org/romanmissal) and find the text for the Eucharistic Prayers. Choose one and use it for meditation and reflection for 15 minutes every day for the next week.

Preface Dialogue

The Eucharistic Prayer begins with a dialogue between the priest and the people. A dialogue is a conversation. The dialogue is followed by the Preface which the priest prays. After the Preface we all sing or say the Holy, Holy, Holy. There are only a few changes to these texts.

Previous Translation	New Translation
PRIEST: The Lord be with you.	**PRIEST**: The Lord be with you.
PEOPLE: And also with you.	**PEOPLE**: And with your spirit.
PRIEST: Lift up your hearts.	**PRIEST**: Lift up your hearts.
PEOPLE: We lift them up to the Lord.	**PEOPLE**: We lift them up to the Lord.
PRIEST: Let us give thanks to the Lord our God.	**PRIEST**: Let us give thanks to the Lord our God.
PEOPLE: It is right to give him thanks and praise.	**PEOPLE**: It is right and just.

Holy, Holy, Holy

The Holy, Holy, Holy comes at a significant time in the Mass. It is just before we ask the Holy Spirit to transform the bread and wine into the Body and Blood of Christ. It is appropriate then to praise God and affirm

What reasons would you offer to explain why "it is right and just" to give thanks to the Lord our God.

his holiness. This very holy prayer is composed of words that all come from the Scriptures. With it we are directly addressing God which is what the entire Eucharistic Prayer does. The Preface concludes by announcing that we are about to proclaim God's majesty together with the angels. In this way, our singing of the Holy, Holy, Holy lifts a universal hymn of praise to God. All of creation sings its theme song, one that comes from the choir of angels and that makes a perfect hymn to praise a holy God.

Previous Translation	New Translation
Holy, holy, holy Lord, God of **power and might.** Heaven and earth are full of your glory. Hosanna in the highest. Blessed is he who comes in the name of the Lord. Hosanna in the highest.	Holy, Holy, Holy Lord God of **hosts.** Heaven and earth are full of your glory. Hosanna in the highest. Blessed is he who comes in the name of the Lord. Hosanna in the highest.

"Holy, Holy, Holy, Lord God of Hosts" are words that Isaiah, the prophet heard the angels singing when they were in God's presence. "Lord God of hosts" was the title that David, the young shepherd called God when he was about to fight the giant Goliath. David said he was talking about the God of the armies of Israel. Hosts can also be heavenly bodies such as angels in God's court. The second part of this prayer reminds us of the praise that the people gave Jesus on Palm Sunday.

Every time we say or sing the Holy, Holy, Holy we join the saints and angels in their song. We are a part of all of creation singing a perfect hymn to praise a holy God.

No matter which of the Eucharistic Prayers the priest says when we listen carefully we will hear and remember all the ways that God has saved us. During the Eucharistic Prayer the whole Church remembers and says thank you for:

> **With a partner or in a small group, look up these verses in the Bible and compare the stories.** Isaiah 6:1-3 1 Samuel 17:1-45 1 Kings 22:19 Revelation 4:8-10 Matthew 21:9

- All God's gifts.
- The gift of Jesus, God's Son.
- Jesus death, his Resurrection, and his Ascension.
- Jesus promise to be with us always

During the Eucharistic Prayer the whole Church remembers and thanks God for all his gifts.

Institution Narrative

Midway through the Eucharistic Prayer the priest prays that the Holy Spirit will make our gifts holy so they become the Body and Blood of Christ. The priest recounts the story of the Last Supper. We call the telling of the story of the Last Supper at Mass the Institution narrative. It is the story of Jesus instituting the Eucharist. Every time we come to Mass we remember what Jesus did for us and what he asked us to do. This is a critical part of Mass, very dear to the heart of Catholics. Usually you can hear the people in church become more attentive as the priest speaks the words of Christ, lifts the consecrated bread and wine, and genuflects in adoration. Some of the words you hear at this time will also change.

Previous Translation	New Translation
Take this, all of you, and eat it: this is my body which will be given up for you.	TAKE THIS, ALL OF YOU, AND EAT OF **FOR** THIS IS MY BODY, WHICH WILL BE GIVEN UP FOR YOU.

Notice that the only difference is the insertion of the words "of" and "for." The meaning is basically the same, but the new translation expresses that we all share some "of" the same bread. By partaking of one bread, we become one body in Christ (see 1 Corinthians 10:17). Furthermore, the reason we share this food is because it is the Body of Christ, given up for us.

REFLECTION QUESTION: Give three concrete examples of how you see the Church being one body in Christ in today's world.

There are more differences in the new translation when the priest repeats the words of Christ, concerning the chalice of wine.

Previous Translation	New Translation
Take this, all of you, and drink from it: this is the **cup** of my blood, the blood of the new and **everlasting** covenant. It will be **shed** for you and for **all so that sins may be forgiven.** Do this in memory of me.	TAKE THIS, ALL OF YOU, AND DRINK FROM IT, **FOR** THIS IS THE **CHALICE** OF MY BLOOD, THE BLOOD OF THE NEW AND **ETERNAL** COVENANT, **WHICH** WILL BE **POURED OUT** FOR YOU AND FOR **MANY FOR THE FORGIVENESS OF SINS.** DO THIS IN MEMORY OF ME.

There are some important words to reflect on in the Institution Narrative:

"Chalice." The use of "chalice" instead of "cup" matches usual way of referring to the vessel on the altar; it highlights the ceremonial use of the vessel even at the Last Supper.

"Covenant." means a promise between two parties. God made a covenant or promise to the people of the Old Testament that he would be their God and they would be his people. When Jesus says "the Blood of the new and eternal covenant," Jesus is saying that by his death on the Cross there is a new promise that he will be with us forever and ever. The use of "eternal" instead of "everlasting" in the new translation is significant because in English, everlasting means something like long-lasting. It refers to something within the confines of time and history. However, eternal cannot be measured in time. God's covenant with us cannot be measured.

"Poured out for you and for many for the forgiveness of sins." means that Jesus' death on the Cross did not just happen to him but he made the choice to do it. "Poured out" is a more active verb than "shed." He wanted people to experience the forgiveness of sins. The new wording makes Jesus' mission of reconciliation clearer.

"For Many." The previous translation says that Jesus shed his blood for all, whereas the new translation says he poured out his blood for many. To some, the new translation will make it sound as though Jesus has had second thoughts about just who and how many would be redeemed. After all, it is clear from several places in the New Testament that Jesus came for the salvation of all (see John 11:52; 2 Corinthians 5:14–15; Titus 2:11; and 1 John 2:2). Nonetheless, the word in Latin literally means "for many," and this is the word that Jesus himself used at the Last Supper, according to Matthew 26:28 and Mark 14:24. It is probably an allusion to Isaiah 53:12, the prophecy about the suffering servant who bore the sin of "many."

During the Institution narrative, through the power of the Holy Spirit and the words and actions of the priest the bread and wine are changed into the Body and Blood of Christ. We call this the consecration.

The words of institution are very important to Catholics. We become more attentive at this part of the Mass.

Memorial Acclamation

After the consecration of the Bread and Wine into the Body and Blood of Christ the priest announces: "The mystery of faith." We affirm that that the risen Christ is with us now and that he will be coming again. We know that all people who love God and do his will, will live with him in heaven when they die. We believe because Jesus promised us. After the priest makes his announcement we make clear that we believe in the mystery of faith. There are three different ways we can make clear or acclaim the mystery of faith:

First Option

We proclaim your Death, O Lord,
and profess your Resurrection
until you come again.

When we profess Christ's Resurrection we are saying we believe he rose from the dead and he lives. We believe he will come again in glory at the end of time.

Second Option

When we eat this Bread and drink
 this Cup,
we proclaim your Death, O Lord,
until you come again.

When we proclaim Christ's death we say publicly that we believe he died on the Cross and he will come again.

Third Option

Save us, Savior of the world,
for by your Cross and Resurrection,
you have set us free.

In this acclamation we say we believe Christ has freed us from sin.

Each of these acclamations is a prayer addressed to Christ. You may remember the response "Christ has died, / Christ is risen, / Christ will come again." It was omitted from the new translation because it was a proclamation *about* Christ rather than an acclamation addressed *to* Christ.

Before the concluding doxology, the priest asks God to accept our sacrifice. He prays that God will make us holy like the saints who are in heaven with him. He reminds us to pray for one another and for the people

> **Read** 1 Corinthians 11:23–26 and write or sketch about what it means for you to act in remembrance of Jesus.
> - On a blank page draw two columns.
> - In the first column write any statements from this chapter that were important for you.
> - In the second column write what they mean to you.

who have died. The Eucharistic Prayer concludes when the priest leads the doxology and the people answer, "Amen."

Doxology

The Eucharistic Prayer ends with the priest praying a prayer of praise to God the Father; through, with, and in Christ; in the unity of the Holy Spirit. This is called a doxology. We respond, "Amen," a word borrowed from Hebrew. Some words express something so perfectly in one language that they never change when they go to another. Many everyday expressions in English are borrowed directly from languages such as Greek (*hoi polloi*), French (*entrepreneur*), Italian (*spaghetti*), and Hebrew (*Alleluia*). The word *Amen* means "So be it"—or even, "I agree" or I believe. It is a holy word that has resisted any further translation. It remains the same.

The doxology proclaims the glory and honor of God.

The doxology of the priest, however, will be slightly different. Soon you will hear these words: "Through him, and with him, and in him, /O God, almighty Father, / in the unity of the Holy Spirit, / all glory and honor is yours, / for ever and ever." The main difference here is the word order, which more nearly imitates the flow of the Latin. It names the three Persons of the Trinity in succession, so it is easier to tell that the prayer is offered to God the Father, through Jesus Christ, and in the Holy Spirit.

The closing of the Eucharistic Prayer is another dialogue between the priest and the people. Just as this prayer opens with a dialogue, so it closes with one. The complete Eucharistic Prayer follows the same structure as the Collect, the Prayer over the Offerings, and the Prayer after Communion. The priest recites the text, and we answer, "Amen." The same is true here. The priest, who has recited most of the words of the Eucharistic Prayer, also proclaims the doxology. Then we reply. Just as we do not sing the doxology with the priest, so he should not sing the "Amen" with us. He proclaims the glory and honor of God, and we answer, "Amen" to his words. We affirm all that has been said before. We call this a great "Amen" because it concludes the greatest prayer of all.

The Communion Rite

During the Communion Rite of the Mass we prepare ourselves to receive the Body and Blood of Christ. The Communion Rite begins with the Lord's Prayer and continues through the Prayer after Communion. What we do before and while receiving Holy Communion does not change. Together we stand and pray the Lord's Prayer. We remember we are one family with God. As a sign of unity we share the Sign of Peace with each other. We receive Holy Communion and we are sent forth. But some of the words will be different when we begin using the new edition of *The Roman Missal*.

Life Experience

Recall a time or event in your family's life or with a group of close friends when you really felt united with them; when you were all in "sync."

Discuss the experience using the following questions as conversation starters:

- What were you doing?
- How did you contribute to the feeling?
- What are the things that break that unity?
- What can you do to increase unity with family and friends?

The Lord's Prayer

After the priest gives a brief invitation, we pray the Lord's Prayer together. The Lord's Prayer has not changed. It is one of the holiest and most well-known of all Christian prayers. In this part of the Mass, most of the changes have been made to the priest's parts. Between the Lord's Prayer and our acclamation ("For the kingdom . . .), the priest will say this prayer

> Deliver us, Lord, we pray, from every evil,
> graciously grant peace in our days,
> that, by the help of your mercy,
> we may be always free from sin
> and safe from all distress,
> as we await the blessed hope
> and the coming of our Savior, Jesus Christ.

Instead of saying, "we wait in joyful hope for the coming of our Savior, Jesus Christ," the priest says, "we await the blessed hope / and the coming of our Savior, Jesus Christ."

His words echo the letter of Saint Paul to Titus 2:13, which affirms that Christ has come and that we await the blessed hope of his return. Christ is our hope. We await his coming—even when we do not feel so joyful.

REFLECTION QUESTION Read Titus 2:11-13 and then write about ways your faith in Jesus Christ helps you when you are sad or worried about something in your life?

Sign of Peace

We exchange the Sign of Peace before receiving Holy Communion. The Sign of Peace is optional, but it is exchanged in almost every Mass. Remember that the Sign of Peace is an action prayer. We reach out our hand to people around us. We wish them God's peace. Giving the Sign of Peace to others is a sign that we are united with one another at the Table of the Lord. We remember we are one family with God.

After the Lord's Prayer, the priest prays to Jesus for peace and unity in the Church:

PRIEST: Lord Jesus Christ,
   who said to your Apostles:
Peace I leave you,
   my peace I give you;
look not on our sins,
but on the faith of
   your Church,
and graciously grant her
   peace and unity
in accordance with
   your will.
Who live and reign for
   ever and ever.

We exchange the Sign of Peace before receiving Holy Communion.

PEOPLE: **Amen.**

In the priest's prayer he calls the Church "her." The Church is our Mother. This prayer reminds us that what Christ wants for the whole Church is peace and unity. In the Gospel according to John, Jesus gives a long talk to his disciples and he tells them that his will for all of his followers is that they will know peace. When the priest greets us, he says:

PRIEST: The peace of the Lord be with you always.

PEOPLE: **And with your spirit.**

Lamb of God

During the breaking of the bread, the priest prays a short prayer as he places a small piece of the consecrated bread into the chalice. While he does that we sing or say the Lamb of God. Lamb of God is a name for Jesus. It reminds us that Jesus died for our sins. When we pray or sing this prayer we remember that through Jesus' death and Resurrection our sins are forgiven and we have peace. There are no changes to the Lamb of God.

Just before we go to receive Holy Communion the priest makes an announcement, and then joins you in the response, "Lord, I am not worthy." Both parts of this dialogue will have some changes.

Previous Translation	New Translation
PRIEST: **This is** the Lamb of God who takes away the sins of the world. **Happy** are those **who are called to his supper.**	**PRIEST**: **Behold** the Lamb of God, **behold him** who takes away the sins of the world. **Blessed** are those **called to the supper of the Lamb.**
ALL: Lord, I am not worthy **to receive you,** but only say the word and **I shall be healed.**	**ALL**: Lord, I am not worthy **that you should enter under my roof,** but only say the word and **my soul** shall be healed.

The words "Lamb of God" also remind us of Jesus' sacrifice on the cross and his presence with us at Mass. They call us to the sacred meal we will share at Communion. It is a great honor to be called to share the Lord's Supper. It is really a gift that we have done nothing to deserve.

Instead of saying, "This is the Lamb of God," the priest will say, "Behold the Lamb of God." This is closer to the Latin, more majestic in sound, and a more direct reference to John 1:29, where John the Baptist points out Jesus to his followers. The word "Happy" has been changed to "Blessed." You may be blessed even when you are experiencing sorrow. This change, together with the explicit reference to "the supper of the Lamb," makes clearer the connection to Revelation 19:9. There, the angel in the vision has John write down the words that proclaim blessed are all those called to the wedding banquet of the Lamb.

> **Read** John 1:24–34 or Revelation 19: 9–10 and sketch a picture of what comes to your imagination as you read.

The reply makes two changes. First, "to receive you" becomes "that you should enter under my roof." This makes a more direct connection with the story of the Centurion in Matthew 8:8 and Luke 7:6, where a Roman Centurion asks Jesus to heal his servant. Jesus intends to go to the house, but the Centurion feels he is unworthy to have Jesus come to his home. Jesus admires the man's faith and cures the servant from afar.

"Lord, I am not worthy / that you should enter under my roof."

We are like the Centurion who asks Jesus to cure his servant. We too, are unworthy to have Jesus come to us but we too have faith and that is what Jesus looks for. By praying the words of the Centurion we tell Jesus of our unworthiness, knowing he will come to us because we believe.

Holy Communion

The priest says a couple of short prayers silently before receiving Holy Communion.

When it is our turn to receive Holy Communion, we cup our hands with one hand on top of the other. The priest or extraordinary minister of Holy Communion says, "The Body of Christ." We answer, "Amen." If we also receive Communion from the cup we answer "Amen" to the words "The Blood of Christ." Our "Amen" confesses our belief that Jesus is truly present in both the bread and the wine. If you choose to received the Body of Christ directly in your mouth, first answer, "Amen," then extend your tongue.

Prayer after Communion

The Communion Rite ends with the Prayer after Communion. The priest invites us to pray the prayer when he says, "Let us pray." Listen to the words the priest prays and respond with "Amen" when he finishes.

> With a partner or in a small group, **look up** and read these verses in the Bible.
> Matthew 8:8 Luke 7:6

We still respond "Amen" to "The Body of Christ."

Write a prayer. In it share your thoughts and feelings about receiving Christ in Holy Communion.

6

The Concluding Rites

Blessing

If there are any brief announcements, they are made before the final blessing. The priest will then greet you as he has been doing, with "The Lord be with you," and you will reply with the response, "And with your spirit." If the priest is using a Prayer over the People or a Solemn Blessing, he or the deacon will invite you to bow your heads as you hear the words. You respond "Amen." As the priest blesses you, he makes the Sign of the Cross over you. You respond again with "Amen."

A blessing is an action that uses words and gestures to ask God to show his kindness to those being blessed. There are many kinds of blessings. The Church blesses people and objects. At Mass

Life Experience

Recall a time or event your life when somethi meaningful happened to y and you wanted to share with your friends becau you wanted them to ha the same experience.
What was the time or even
• Why did you think it was important to share it?
• How did you share it?
• How did the people you shared it with respond?

46